quiet

night

think

ALSO BY GILLIAN SZE

POETRY

Fish Bones
The Anatomy of Clay
Peeling Rambutan
Redrafting Winter
Panicle

PICTURE BOOKS

The Night Is Deep and Wide
My Love for You Is Always
You Are My Favorite Color

GILLIAN SZE

quiet

night

think

poems & essays

Published by ECW Press
665 Gerrard Street East
Toronto, Ontario, Canada M4M 1Y2
416-694-3348 / info@ecwpress.com

Editor for the Press: Michael Holmes /
a misFit Book
Copy-editor: Emily Schultz
Cover design: Jessica Albert

MISFIT

LIBRARY AND ARCHIVES CANADA CATALOGUING
IN PUBLICATION

Title: Quiet night think : poems & essays / Gillian Sze.

Names: Sze, Gillian, 1985- author.

Identifiers: Canadiana (print) 20210349212 |
Canadiana (ebook) 20210349271

ISBN 978-1-77041-625-3 (softcover)
ISBN 978-1-77305-925-9 (ePub)
ISBN 978-1-77305-926-6 (PDF)
ISBN 978-1-77305-927-3 (Kindle)

Classification: LCC PS8637.Z425 Q54 2022 | DDC
C811/.6—dc23

We acknowledge the support of the Canada Council for the Arts. *Nous remercions le Conseil des arts du Canada de son soutien.* This book is funded in part by the Government of Canada. *Ce livre est financé en partie par le gouvernement du Canada.* We acknowledge the support of the Ontario Arts Council (OAC), an agency of the Government of Ontario, which last year funded 1,965 individual artists and 1,152 organizations in 197 communities across Ontario for a total of $51.9 million. We also acknowledge the support of the Government of Ontario through the Ontario Book Publishing Tax Credit, and through Ontario Creates.

ONTARIO ARTS COUNCIL
CONSEIL DES ARTS DE L'ONTARIO
an Ontario government agency
un organisme du gouvernement de l'Ontario

Canada Council   Conseil des arts
for the Arts   du Canada

Canadä

This book is for my family,
especially my mother and father—
I sing for you.

CONTENTS

INSTRUCTIONS

When I say *yellow*,
fold yourself.
Lose count of geese.
Measure seeds
by placing them between your lips
and humming.
A walnut lets out an opera.
Observe the cypress in full sunlight.
Do so again in old age.
If it grows bright,
pay homage.
If it grows dark,
bargain at will.
The fern is another word
for memory.
Watch the clouds
as they knit their way
across the night.
What I want to tell you
is imperative—
that we are flawed
and exalted,
that there are those
who still look to the raven for rain.
When the wind
pines through your window,
let it.
The wind misses you.
It misses
everything
about
you.

QUIET NIGHT THINK

There is a famous poem, written by Li Bai in the eighth century, which has long been taught to schoolchildren in China. It goes as follows:

床前明月光，
疑是地上霜。
举头望明月，
低头思故乡。

Before my bed, the moon is shining bright,
I think that it is frost upon the ground.
I raise my head and look at the bright moon,
I lower my head and think of home.

Written in the form of a quatrain, each line five characters long, the poem conveys the speaker's yearning for home while gazing at the moon.[1] All this is done in twenty characters. There have been innumerable translations of this poem and this particular version manages to succeed in thirty-five words. Chinese poetry tends to be economical and pithy. To translate from a language that typically removes articles and pronouns is no simple task. Consider, for instance, the title of the poem, 靜夜思 [Jìng Yè Sī], which means literally "Quiet Night Think." Some translators supply "Thinking on a Quiet Night," others "Quiet Night Thoughts," or even a singular "A Quiet Night Thought." Some have taken more liberal and creative routes, and so the poem is variously entitled: "Contemplating Moonlight," "Brooding in the Still Night," or "Lamentations in the Tranquility of Night." Evidently, the Chinese title bears no mention of moonlight or lamentation. Most Chinese people simply understand "Quiet Night Think" as "nostalgia."

Anyone who has been nostalgic would agree that nostalgia is often a product of night, silence, thought, and yes, probably moonlight.

When I first learned this poem, I was six. I attended Saturday Chinese school in Winnipeg and had to have the poem memorized for a recitation competition the following week. While it was easy enough to remember (only twenty characters long and following a catchy AABA rhyme scheme) I wanted, more than anything, to know what it was *about*. I could recite the poem perfectly in Mandarin—both tonally and rhythmically, incorporating even that unwritten pause that separates the first two syllables from the latter three in each line—but I could see that in English, my stronger language, something was missing. After converting each monosyllabic Chinese character into an English counterpart, I still could not make out the sense. The lines became:

bed front bright moon light
suspect is ground on frost
raise head look bright moon
low head think hometown.

My mother, who sat with me at the dining room table, struggled to translate. She would repeat a word from the poem, as if murmuring it again and again in Chinese could somehow locate it in English. Then she would pause and hold her breath as if she was nearing it, but all that came out was air. A frustrated burst of breath.

Only now do I see that what I was asking my mother to do was not translate the text, word for word, but to translate poetry, which is a different thing entirely. William Carlos Williams defines a poem as "a thing made up of . . . words and the spaces between them."[2] What I was demanding of my mother was to translate that space, to string together for me the twenty blocks into poetry. Between her scant English and my dogged determination to pry meaning out of her, we found ourselves caught in the middle of words and languages. Our stuttering search for precision led only to the disappointment that I couldn't feel the same sway from the poem as she did.

What is this space that poetry offers? Creative space. Emotional space. Reflective space. A space for possibilities. The poem, for a long time, remained a rigid slab of words with no room to make the leap. I wanted space, but I didn't know then that to gain it, you have to lose something. Loss, as my mother already knew, is what provides the space from which meaning can emerge.

What takes place between the third and fourth line, between lifting one's head to the moon and then bowing? A lot. Li Bai knows how that space is filled. While revered as one of the best Tang Dynasty poets, Li Bai is a bit of a mystery with uncertain origins (some say he is from the Sichuan province, some say he may have been Turkic). Many transliterations of his name exist so he is also Li Po, Li Pai, or Li T'ai-po. Ezra Pound, in *Cathay*, even refers to the Chinese poet as Rihaku, the Japanese rendering of his name.

Li Bai had opportunities, presumably, for nostalgia. A Confucian scholar, a Daoist hermit, a soldier, and a drunk, Li Bai led a life of movement. He searched for patrons and listeners. Eventually recognized for his poetic genius, he was appointed by the emperor and brought to the capital of Chang'an, but was later expelled (he was drunk once again in court but this time got in trouble for it). His wandering continued until he died.

Of course, I only learned this later when I was older and came across a book of Chinese verse and was reminded of the poem. At the time, when I was sitting at the dining room table with my mother, I didn't know anything about what it meant to look up on a quiet night when the moonlight hit the floor in front of my bed. In five words *(bed front bright moon light)*, Li Bai tells us exactly where the moon is, how brightly it comes in, where it eventually lands. The moment is so specific. For anyone who has seen this light (and here I think of Emily Dickinson's famous first line, "There's a certain Slant of light"), this moment is so familiar. *Heavenly Hurt, it gives us.*

My mother knows about the moon. Born in a village in the south of China, she promptly shucked the country and grew up in the French district of Shanghai. I've seen black-and-white photos of her there with braids down to her hips, riding a bicycle, or leaning out of her balcony. During the revolution, she, like many others, was sent away to work on the farms. Much too rural for a city girl. When I visited China in 2008, I followed my mother and saw the small house where she had briefly stayed. It was a hot day and we clutched parasols to save us from the sun. Inside the home was cool and upon entering, I looked up to see a portrait of my great-grandmother hanging high from the wooden beam. So much happens between lifting one's head and then lowering it. My mother looked up and said nothing. Sometimes there are just spaces. Sometimes brightness doesn't have anywhere to land.

I started work on my book *Peeling Rambutan* soon after I returned from China. By then I had seen many different moons: on a bus rumbling down to my parents' villages, in Hong Kong as I roamed the city hunting for temples, after a late dinner at a Mamak stall in Kuala Lumpur. So much is carried through moonlight. Though I have been gone nearly twenty years, I still think that the moon looks most natural when it lands in the backyard of my childhood home.

The epigraph that opens *Peeling Rambutan* is a poem not by Li Bai, but his contemporary, Wang Wei. I found it while reading about emptiness in Chinese poetry.

> empty mountain / not see people
> but hear /people speak / sound
> returning light / enter deep wood
> again shine / green moss / top[3]

Until then, I had only read translations already rounded out and smoothed over in English. Suddenly, the word-for-word version was no longer obscure but became a relief and a comfort. The breaks in each line reminded me of the fractured dialects I grew up with, the skipping from language to language, the acrobatic ear. "The poem does not tell the reader much," scholar Ming Dong Gu writes of Wang Wei, and continues, "it is practically blank."[4] The slashes marked off empty space—space that was poetic and necessary. Wang Wei's poem reminded me of the recurring conversations I had with my family's ghosts while an ocean away, as I tried to put together some hiccupped notion of home. I recognized the faltering English as my own.

In my first attempt to understand Li Bai, when I asked my mother to translate, I took the wrong approach and stubbornly relied on literality for meaning. After she explained the first line, I foolishly asked, "But where does it say 'window'? How do you know that there's a window?" Exasperated, she switched from Mandarin to our own dialect, Hokkien, and said, "Of course there's a window! How else could the moonlight come in?"

★

They say Li Bai wandered until he died at the age of sixty-two. There are many stories about how he died, but this one is the most famous. He was drunk. Unfortunately, he was also in a boat. The moon was reflected in the water and, in his stupor, he attempted to embrace it. Instead of looking up, this time Li Bai looked down to see the pale orb floating closer than it had ever been. I wonder what he was thinking then. Arms wide, he stumbled into the moon and drowned.

FAUNA

Somewhere
it unravels,
lands furled upon moss,

snagged in the spider's web,
or sits dewed upon long blades of morning.

It breaks dormancy
roots and shoots
to meet tinselled cheeps
and the uncertain step of a fawn.

At each point

where cygnets touch nest, touch water,
or horns graze birch and brush,

is a whisper that flits forward,
glow upon glow,
affirming what's buried beneath.

No one tells you
that the ark was made of light
each cubit knotted and dazzled

and while the world was daring to die
from each icicle and sprig

they came, two and two,
in them the breath of light.

PRAYER

Trimmed baby hairs tossed in the backyard
now curl in a nest.

Moss limes the bark.
Beneath the sudden rays, ice laces the heads of hedges.

The glaucous leaves of the carnations are fringed with melting snow.
When did they find the time to survive?

It's almost May and we're still lamenting
the languid spell of winter.

When panicked, grant me
the unshakable calm of flowers.

TEN TRANSITIONS
after 思恺

Welcoming Spring

The thunderstorm comes at night; what's left of the snow disappears.
By bright morning, the bushes flutter with colourful finches.

Audacity

Dozens of children delight in the piano inside the ice cream shop.
One by one, they bend and plunk the keys. Beams of sound warm the room.

Tomorrow's Spring Equinox

For a few days, the sky warmed up. Leftovers of ice and snow.
Yesterday, a hurricane touched down, sweeping the yard and burying boots.
Leaves green, flowers flower, and yet the branches are bald.
How common the unexpected. How elusive both luck and mishap.

Ontario Sleet

Rain dropped in the night, glazing the cables and branches with ice.
Disaster sparkles, translucent. So many are cold, so cold.

Visiting Burrard Inlet

A skiff slowly leaves the shore. The city's beauty sprawls before me,
as if the jade halls suddenly became earthbound and I stare out from Buddha's peak.
A thousand hectares of ripples lead to the sea, carrying ten thousand tons of cargo.
A biting breeze blows past. My heart scorches like the hottest day in China.

Out and About

When the grey rain lingers, go out and buy vegetables.
Handpick lotus roots and winter melon. Drag your brimming trolley home.

Thoughts on Reading Poems

The old neighbours are complaining: the melons in the yard—wasted again.
Born from the frigid air of the north, the snow geese will not return to the nest.

First Day of Autumn

Summer recedes once again for autumn, receiving the maple and the cardinal.
The grizzled and golden wind is keen with meaning; the seasons—too short to be selfish.

Squamish, B.C.

The cable car angles for the mountaintop. Summer takes in a full breath. Forest, verdant pine, stands tall, while the sun waits on snow peaks. The stream makes its way seaward. The mellow wind sweeps over it all. A shadow leans against the railing. My granddaughter's arms open, seeking. I stoop, wary, an aged bull beside the calf.

Snow Festival

A cold wave overwhelms, and nothing can pierce the soil.
The pool cools the bones and seagulls play tricks.
In the distance, the slopes of snow-capped mountains are gilded.
Daylight is brief; tomorrow morning, read this again, carefully.

TO DRAW WATER

The traditional Chinese practice of naming dates back to the Shang Dynasty (1600–1046 BC), during China's Bronze Age. The elders of a family would first compose a short verse called a generation poem. Each word in the poem corresponds to a single generation and makes up part of a family member's name, which is typically composed of two Chinese characters. With each emerging generation, the poem moves forward a word, following the established sequence.

In time, as family members spring up, buds shooting forth one after the other, they eventually find themselves winding around that final line break and proceeding to the last word. Once that happens, the poem can be repeated from the beginning again, or extended with new verse. Poems and lineages are recorded, leaving space in anticipation. There is plenty of time to accommodate future progeny and to consider the next line. A single iteration of a poem forty-two characters long, for example, can last a family just over a thousand years, assuming they procreate successfully every thirty years.

The intimacy of the family becomes the intimacy of a poem, lines and lineages memorized. In a village, one could hear another's name, know to which family and generation he belonged, and determine immediately his seniority within a clan, as well as who his brother, father, and grandfather are just based on an excerpted phrase. A making of sense. To have a name was to be part of a poem, alive and engaged with words before and always in wait for words to come.

My name did not follow a poem. It was chosen first in English by my mother and then reduced from its three syllables to two possible sounds. Each sound became a Chinese character. Here I run into the delight of homophones. In Mandarin, a single sound can be shared by over one hundred characters. Its tone, of which there are four, can narrow the sound down to almost forty possible characters. How can we understand each other? Three things certainly help. The first is that, as with anything, mastery over time is possible. The second is that language depends on context. And the third is that often the sound of a character needs to be joined to the sound of another in order to produce meaning, otherwise on its own, it will be senseless. Even in pairs, sounds can continue to reverberate throughout the language. For example, the characters for "banana" (xiāngjiāo: 香蕉) sound the same as the verb "to make friends" (xiāngjiāo: 相交). It is the trick, or slip, that occurs in any language.

When constructing our names, my mother used our English names as a constraint. She translated sounds from one language to another. When said aloud, my Chinese name sounds recognizably like its English counterpart. The first character of my name, *jí*, means "lucky." One look for its Pinyin (the romanized spelling of the Chinese pronunciation) in a dictionary will reveal that it shares the same sound as the words for "stammer," "urgent," "to draw (water)," and "to gather." The second character, *lían*, refers to the lotus flower. *Lían* can also mean: "scythe," "ripple," "a hanging screen or curtain," and "to connect."

I often think of the poetic work that goes into a name. Those careful tasks of composing, testing, titling, and finding the compatibility between meaning and resonance, sound and connotation. My Chinese name placed me in a matrix of homophones, a riddle of notes composed of varying levels of coherence. I was part of a constellation, one among many possible significations. As I grew older, I saw myself as a book that my mother was first responsible for naming.

★

My father delighted in second-hand books. He sought them out at garage sales and libraries. He would go to St. Vital Centre, the nearest mall to us in Winnipeg, where the Children's Hospital Foundation regularly held a fundraising book sale. He would return home with stacks of old *National Geographic*s, Reader's Digest Condensed Books, books on finances and retirement, and various travel guides. Everything, he boasted, was between twenty-five cents and a dollar.

My first collection of poems that still sits on my shelf was found in this bounty. Its cover was yellowed and the edges of the pages were clearly worn and handled (presumably by an "L. Russell," whose name was written inside). On the cover was a dizzying pink image of an abstract painting, reminiscent of the technique children use when capturing the symmetry of butter-flies. At the top right corner, the words: *20th-Century Poetry & Poetics*. I opened it and my eyes widened at the lines by Cohen: "As you undress you sing out, and your voice is magnificent / because now you believe it is the first human voice / heard in that room."⁵ I was fourteen.

This collection of poems was my first encounter with Sylvia Plath, Wallace Stevens, William Carlos Williams, as well as bpNichol, Al Purdy, and Margaret Avison. I read Roethke's remarks on rhyme, Yeats's on symbolism, and essays by the Roberts (Creeley, Frost, Graves, Lowell). I memorized Auden's "As I Walked Out One Evening" for no other reason than wanting to have the hyper-bolic declaration of love in the third and fourth stanza always in my reach.

My earliest teachers of poetry were the rhymes and songs encountered in grade school. But *20th Century Poetry & Poetics*—read during that age of easy impressions and earliest desires—was what kept me up, what moved me, what steeled me with love and nerve.

★

Homophonous sounds in English can make for those puns that elicit chuckles from some but groans and eye rolls from most. Chinese puns, on the other hand, are taken very seriously. A whole country will alter its diet on certain holidays for the sake of a pun. In Mandarin, there is a common idiom uttered during the Chinese New Year. 年年有余 (*Nián nián yǒu yú*) means "there will be an abundance every year." But the fourth character shares the same sound as the word for "fish," and so it can also mean: "there will be fish every year." As a result, fish takes on the sense of surplus and becomes a feature dish during new year dinner.

It doesn't take much to change the vector of meaning, to see homonyms shoot out from a Catherine wheel in various colours, speeds, and vibrancy. In a Sinitic language, a single alteration to a character's tone will change its course. The new word roars past and seeks new territory. Sometimes that word moves alone.

The number four is a linguistic pariah among the Chinese. In Mandarin, when the character for "four" is pronounced in a different tone (of which the dialect has four), it sounds like "death." This occurs similarly in Cantonese, a six-tone dialect. The near-homophone of "four" is scattered throughout the number system in various ways, puncturing the mere task of counting with darkness. The number fourteen in Cantonese sounds similar to "must die." Twenty-four can mean "easy to die," and 514 sounds like "I want to die." The number four, needless to say, is unlucky, even if it only skirts the sound of death.

Nevertheless, the sounds of words are powerful enough to affect things like architecture, public transportation, and coordinates. In Hong Kong, where Cantonese is used, some apartments skip the fourth floor, as well as the fourteenth, and everything between floors 39 and 50. In Taiwan, house numbers that end with the number four are also skipped, as are bus number plates in Singapore and phone numbers in China.

While "four" sounds like "death," "eight," on the other hand, is a near-homophone for "fortune" (and all of its cognates). If the number four can alter the organization of a city in an attempt to avoid death, then the number eight makes everyone move in the other direction with the same weight of superstition. For example, China was happy to host the 2008 Olympics because of the presence of the number eight in the year, a lucky number. The opening games took place, not coincidentally, at 8:08 p.m. on the eighth day, of the eighth month.[6] Eight is desirable for everything from wedding dates and birthdays to cellphone numbers and licence plates. An airline in China paid $280,000 in order to secure the phone number 88888888.[7] Some even say that the large Asian population in Los Angeles's San Fernando Valley is due to the auspicious area code 818.

Why is 818 a good number? It is a near-homophone for the phrase "prosper and prosper." My parents' first home in Winnipeg had the number 818. There is a picture of them standing proudly on the front steps.

★

What are you trying to be? Western? my father said. I had just been told that I couldn't attend the school dance. His rhetorical quip baffled me, not knowing how to respond at age twelve when, being born landlocked in the middle of the continent, *the West* was all around me. And yet, always that inescapable underlay of another country beneath our feet, a ghost asleep in the open yawn of the wok, the deft pluck of our chopsticks at my mother's dumplings. My father once told me that in the fastened words of my hyphenated identity, "Chinese" came first. What I heard sounded like *duty, outsider, order, difference.*

For a long time, I struggled with my parents' stories, their endeavours, and the alienation they experienced upon arriving in a new country. I was compelled to find or make meaning out of it all. Writing, while significant to me, felt wayward. Aside from my high school English teacher who encouraged me to seek mentorship with the Manitoba Writers' Guild (too frivolous, I thought at the time) and the librarian (who started a short-lived book club because I was the only student in attendance), no one knew the earnestness with which I wrote.

I remained quiet. What I think my father wanted most was to make a sound, reverberating across the slow prairies, and to hear me make—if not the same sound—at least something close enough that he could consider an echo.

Here is a story about misunderstanding. My parents visited my father's cousin for the first time in Australia. When they arrived, she asked my father what he usually ate for breakfast. He assured her that he was not particular and, in fact, ate oatmeal every morning. She misheard him and thought that instead of "oatmeal," he had said "white pigeon." In Hokkien, the words differ only slightly. My father's cousin panicked and, for the rest of the day, worried that she would be a poor host. Where could she find white pigeon for him? How does one cook it for breakfast?

In order to remain polite and avoid any awkward interrogation, she took my parents to the market and encouraged my father to pick up white pigeon. And so he did. He returned and, much to his cousin's relief, held in his hand a bag of oats.

The Chinese tradition of naming through poetry has waned in the last 3600 years. Migration, cultural revolutions, encounters with difference, passing time—among a myriad of factors—weakened the practice. At its root, the generation poem pertained only to male lineage. (Only in modern practice has that changed. Even then, the female line is organized by its own separate text.)

When following the generation poem, male siblings and their paternal male cousins would inevitably share the Chinese character allotted to their generation. While some of my father's distant relatives still use the poem for naming, his own family, for undisclosed reasons, didn't. My paternal grandfather's name stopped at the poem's seventeenth character. The tradition was inevitably lost when my father crossed the ocean to start anew. Nevertheless, my mother decided to keep a common character in both my brothers' Chinese names. (She even went so far as translating this phenomenon into English and named them Edmond and Edwin.)

I asked my mother where her own family poem went and she said, "I have no idea what it even is. I'm sure it's recorded somewhere back in the village. Women were married off, so their poems don't matter anyway."

While poetry has lost its grip on my family's naming practices, there is no shortage of puns. The widely circulated story about how my mother and her sisters were named uses her as the punchline.

My mother comes from a family of seven sisters. When the fourth daughter was born, my grandfather turned to my grandmother and said that they were done. That was it. And so my aunt was given the name *An An*, meaning "peaceful." *An An* is also a homonym for "that's it." When the fifth daughter was born, my grandfather said that the family was "finished," and, in the same manner, she was named homonymously *Wan Wan*. The characters in her name actually refer to a circle, suggesting perfection. By the time my mother was born, now the sixth daughter in a string of girls, my grandfather threw his hands up and said, "Stop!" As a result, my mother's name, *Ting Ting*, which means "graceful," also happens to have the same sound as *stop*.

My father, like many of my uncles and cousins who immigrated to Canada, came to study. When he arrived in Vancouver in the seventies from Hong Kong, he held an assortment of jobs while putting himself through university. A truck would pick him up at Fortieth and Main and he would ride to a farm where he picked strawberries and potatoes. He was a dishwasher in Gastown and a short-order cook at various hotel restaurants. He finally landed a regular, well-paying summer job, which he always spoke of with some nostalgia. He worked as a waiter for CN Rail and would serve passengers while the changing country, from Vancouver to Montreal, flashed outside the windows.

When it was my turn to start postsecondary studies, I entered a pre-med program and attended classes and labs at the University of Winnipeg. Medicine was a sensible choice. I had made a sound decision. So when an opportunity came up at the beginning of the semester to register for a creative writing course, I didn't mention that I dropped calculus and traded it for a three-hour-long prose seminar. I continued to attend my other classes dutifully, and so convinced myself that this was an immaterial adjustment.

But after my first year, I left Winnipeg and the pre-med program to pursue creative writing and the study of literature in Montreal. This decision did not come with blessings or ease. My relatives considered the humanities a downgrade. My father took it as a personal affront, the idea of becoming a writer simply unheard of and outrageous. For many days, those I left remained disappointed and silent. Long after my departure, I would look west and recognize a breach.

You will come back, my father had said grimly before tying his shoes for work, just hours before I had to catch my flight east. Later when I looked out the window of the plane, I saw only clouds.

★

What's left? The usual: coincidences, contradictions, and irony.

Soon after the golden age of Chinese poetry, the Tang Dynasty, during which nearly 50,000 poems were composed, the Mongolian invasion and rule in the thirteenth century led to poetry's temporary decline. Confucian scholars and poets, once elite members of society, dropped in rank and were placed ninth on the social ladder, between prostitutes and beggars.

    And yet poetry continued. At a temple in Hong Kong, I kneeled and shook my cup of fortune sticks. Each stick is numbered and corresponds to a short poem, which serves as the answer to one's question. This practice dates back to the third century, and it still amazes me to think of all these people flocking to a holy place to read poems, to have poetry provide an answer, to interpret, to allot poetry this much power over their lives.

    I don't fail to see the irony that it was my father who purchased my first book of poetry for a dollar at the mall. Or that in our family's abandoned generation poem, my father's and my generation correspond to two sounds, which are necessarily paired together to mean "freedom" (自由, *zì yóu*). As I write this, I think it perfect that in Mandarin, "memory" (忆, *yi*), "art" (乇, *yi*), and "meaning" (意, *yi*) are homonyms. That to remember, to summon up, and to find meaning is always to engage in something creative.

For some, a poem organizes a family. Such a poem is carried around with a person. It is part of his identity, already decided and embedded in verse. Others can map him, put him against time and other people. He is part of a bloodline, a poetic line, and everyone can anticipate what is uttered next.

    I would be lying to say that I am not enchanted by this system of order and classification. But, as in most poems I read and compose,

I end up searching for its shifts and pauses. What if the next line meanders? Where does a word break off?

In a poem that can only repeat or be extended, how does one misstep—purposefully and without misgiving? The possibility of containment, in any text and like many things in life we try to keep anchored, can't hold. Things fall apart. A fissure ceases to be a flaw. It becomes a new possibility, a new measure, and if the wound is right, sometimes we can draw water. Sometimes we can sing.

SEIZE

Cardinals help me make it through the winter. It's their red plumes against the snow, a flame catching from one branch to another. The cardinal rests like a steady light on the fence in moments of unbeckoned bravery. I feel responsible: watch out for neighbourhood cats and rap on the glass when I have to. The white and grey of the season stretches past my backyard, into the days and months. I am convinced, at times, that the cardinal is all I have left. My belly grows and I wrap myself in wool and pashmina, protect it from the frost and the toothed wind of January. I anticipate summer where new eyes blink, confused by the sudden colour.

MULTIVERSE
for M.S.

She touches a hand to my belly and tells me that I will learn something new about love. *It's another dimension*, she says. We are in a bar where everyone is downing beer, and I thirst for the cold familiar taste of summer. There is still snow on the ground. Everyone has started early; I feel doubly stalled. Recently, you told me some physicists believe our world is only one possibility. That elsewhere, other planets, other universes, other dimensions, exists every other possibility imaginable. When we die, our consciousness bifurcates and jumps from *here* to *there*. *We're immortal*, you said, awed. The baby moves. After seven months, I've come to know how it turns restlessly at night or jigs in the morning after coffee. There is, for now, only one possibility—each motion you've put in me singular and unrepeatable.

YARD WORK

I clear the yard of dead stalks, last year's leaves, dry needles. I move slowly beneath the April sunlight, gathering relics of winter into garbage bags. Lately, a small grey cat has been tiptoeing through the snow-pressed grass. I discover a bowl of milk next to the house. Today the cat creeps out from beneath a shadow, alert and cautious. It watches me, uncertain, and I want to laugh at my own harmlessness. I am eight months pregnant, the most sluggish of predators, catching my breath at the top of the steps. If there is anything in me that makes the cat dart into the hedges and peer out unblinkingly, I do not know what. Perhaps it detects you, the small unseen body that squirms beneath my ribs. The independent mystery —beyond the cat, beyond me.

NURSERY

These days, I am overwhelmed by the task of constructing a world. To prepare a space for you, or maybe to prepare you for what's already out here. You float in me, in want of nothing, oblivious to the evening news, the pilot, who, just the other day, simply aimed for the mountainside. Oblivious to all of the stolen girls, the bounty of heartache. Lately, your father's rage curls around my feet. My nose now bleeds when I cry. Even our home suffers from insomnia and a domestic rhythm that can edge on boredom. I sit on the floor and select what I can to urge you forward without falsehood. *Here is the colour green. Here is the delayed tang of cranberries on the tongue. Here is the rough bark of a fallen branch. Here is a feather, light enough to articulate the stillness of the air.*

PERENNIALS

In the spring, I would lose my mother to gardens.

I, smaller and graceless, would stay inside reading, trying and failing to keep sight of her through the window. Eventually, she'd emerge from between the scented chests of lilac bushes, or straighten up with the irises. Plum blossoms caught in her hair. Dirt in the creases of her wrists.

We had a vegetable garden in our backyard that my mother tended diligently year after year. From the ground, she reaped tomatoes, green beans, zucchinis, scallions, and chives. The garden was shaded by the apple tree growing beside it, which would pop out small fistfuls of apples, sour enough that we couldn't eat them straight. My mother would collect them to make applesauce or just boil them sliced with sugar. She never grew carrots. She told me that with one look at the soil we had, she knew it was too clayish for carrots to grow straight down, so she never bothered.

The garden found its way into our meals and my mother's swiftness with all things made their move from the soil to the sink to the stove unexceptional. She, like my grandmother, whooshed through the home like breath, barely audible, imperceptible as things just got done, or replenished, sewn, and fixed. Returning home from school, I would open the back gate and see my mother crouched over the garden, her feet balanced on a plank of wood, shoulders working as she wrested weeds from earth's hold. Her gloved hands would toss them onto the grass. From the back, her bent knees jutted out like wings.

My mother was always weeding. Our home was nestled in a bend on a boulevard so we had a fairly large plot of grass. While I recall weed killer and specific instructions to keep off the grass for some time, I would still find my mother in the warmer months, bent over, combing through and isolating the unwanted from the acceptable growth.

★

When I finally had my own yard to tend, I had hopes that I would create some lush oasis behind our new home. I received a head start from the person who previously lived there. There was a small peony tree in the front yard, a flowerbed by the stoop, and another one along the walk leading up. Behind the house was a peony bush that poked out from beside a row of tall hedges. There were even empty pots in the shed, waiting to be filled, and four small plots in the backyard for herbs. It took me the first few weeks to realize that my attempts at maintenance were slovenly and, slowly, I came to plant grass.

Indoor plants I could always maintain and nurture. But I soon learned that I couldn't keep up with, let alone combat, the elements. The peony tree didn't survive our first winter in the house. It emerged from beneath the snow a brittle and jagged sight. It was a sad rough draft of spring and never flowered. I had removed the overgrown and unusable herbs the season before and the plots remained vacant, inviting neighbourhood cats to come by and relieve themselves. I replaced the flowerbed along the driveway with rocks because whatever I planted was soon trampled on by visitors who got out of their car and stepped immediately onto a flower, or by trick-or-treaters who tore through the flowerbed in the dark. While I managed to fill the flowerpots in the back—my mother transplanted my grandmother's calla lilies and assured me that this perennial would be easy to maintain—it became clear that I had become a grower of grass. I threw seeds like blessings and replaced the waiting gaps with mere shoots.

★

In her book about gardening, Catherine Abbott warns: "Do not avoid weeding. Putting off weeding is often a new gardener's downfall because weeds can grow rapidly, and before you know it, they are taking over."[8] Our home, located at the bottom of a sloping street, was cupped by spirea bushes. Our yard easily collected the dandelion fluff from neighbouring homes. Soon, yellow buds were shooting up, along with pickle plants and crabgrass that netted over the rocks where the flowerbed once was. I found myself prodded by the writer: "Always remove weeds before they go to seed so they do not have a chance to spread!" Or, "Getting on your hands and knees is probably the best way to get rid of it." Everything felt like an emergency.

Soon weeding became something that worked itself into my life. Upon returning home from the library, or the coffee shop where I laboured over a manuscript, I would pluck a few strays before entering the home and toss them onto the sidewalk where they shrivelled by dusk. But I noticed that once I bent down to start, it was hard to stop. My bag would drop to the ground and I would be on my knees—as recommended by the gardener—scrabbling through the grass. A few yellow heads soon became a pile. I'd step back and admire the uniformity of grass and rock. I became obsessed once I began, urged by the satisfaction of pulling each stalk so wholly that the roots would lift up the soil with each tug

You know, they'll just keep coming back, my husband said as he stood over me shaking his head. His shadow fell over my hands grasping at the unwanted shoots. Something moved me still, out of impulse, out of necessity. *Why do you write?* was a question that I was often asked, and my answer for both weeding and writing was Rilkean: *I must.* Yes, there was something inherently futile with every weed I pulled, but I did so stubbornly, thinking of what Mordecai Richler said: *Each novel is a failure or there would be no compulsion to begin again.*[9] I accepted this mundane hell of always starting over, condemned both at my desk and in my yard. I stuck to weeding the same way I stuck to writing, even after the countless number of people—often baffled family members—asking me what I was going to do with words. *How will you survive on poetry?*

★

There are moments that happen only when the sun is low in the sky and the noises of neighbourhood children begin to fade that I feel the overlay of my own childhood press down on the present. It isn't intrusive, but it is palpable. It is, in short, just a sensation that I carry with me.

Near my childhood home, Kirkbridge Park had a small circular bike path that, when I was young, felt expansive. It seemed to stretch from one end of the world to the other, and there would be races and circuits that left one gasping, small legs aching from pumping the pedals. My favourite length of the path was flanked by marshy grass that hid the sounds of frogs and crickets. The long blades pierced the evening sky, coloured both by exhilarated freedom and the inescapable bike ride back home. In truth, the bike path was really very walkable. I discovered this only when I got older.

Tangential to the path was a short stretch of pavement that ended at the top of a small hill. It was known in the neighbourhood to be a risky drop on a bike, which was probably why the path wasn't extended any further. Construction had stopped but the half-made path wasn't removed for years, which tempted kids to zip down. The acceleration often led to wobbly front wheels and an unavoidable tumble at the bottom.

I thought of this hill when I was in my own yard working, once again, on the weeds. What was the motive behind all this clearing? I wanted to fill a page with words just as I wanted to free my yard of weeds. To write, to begin writing anew, always made sense to me in a way that I couldn't put forth myself. *Motive*, as Nicole Brossard understands it, is something that "eternally returns in the work of an artist. The motive is roots, flesh, and skin."[10] It made one question themselves endlessly, *why?* or, *how come?* Any gardener would have echoed my husband and told me that weeding without tools was ineffective. I chose to use, at most, gloves. I needed to be close to the ground so I could grip, again and again, the taproot. To pull up, again and again, nothing but dirt clinging to new white rootlets.

What made me circle the park, round and round, learning over the years the bumps to avoid and the dangerous dips that could catch a wheel? What compelled me and the other children to return to the top of that hill and whiz down with our bare knees and soft palms? I still am not sure.

I started pulling weeds when I was six months large with my son. With each passing week, I could feel time begin to narrow. As I completed the final edits to a manuscript and wrote the last chapters of my dissertation in order to beat an increasingly real biological deadline, I weeded with ferocity. One evening, I returned from a walk and, once again, found myself sifting through the grass. A Sisyphean task. At one point, belly full of baby, I pulled and fell backwards to the ground.

The next morning, I woke to a sharp twinge that ruptured the early quiet. I went straight into labour. Our street was closed for a city-wide bicycle marathon and we had to call an ambulance to pull us from the stream of cyclists, who rode past the open doors of the ambulance shouting, *Félicitations!* I waved back at them from the gurney. A neighbour, looking down from her balcony, would tell my mother the following week: *One day I saw her weeding, then the next day, the ambulance came!*

★

After sleepless months of adjusting to a new person and the seemingly endless repetition of diapers and baths and nursing, the warmer season returned. I was delivered, once again, to the time of weeds. The squirmy newborn was now stumbling on two feet. My son would wobble between my legs as we moved forward together, his two hands in mine. The urgencies between us were different. Grassy afternoons, I would spread a blanket out for us and try to read, or jot notes. I tugged at words that were intractable. The next book felt like both a failure and a dream. My son became the most tangible thing in my world and I followed his patterns, lived by his schedule, slept—or didn't—when permitted. Outside, the blanket could hardly keep him, and I would wander off with him, barefoot and cautious.

I tried to weed. At the very least, I thought, I could snap off the yellow heads before they clouded over. I thought I could even include my son in this ritual. When able, I appreciated the grip of stalk and, however briefly, held tight to something that was my own. But a pen. A book. Those things became harder to reach in the early months when my son squirmed his way into the centre. I saw then, amidst the repetitions of his daily life, how our home emanated concentric cycles, each of varying needs, time, gravity, and possibility. I circled in all of the orbits—sometimes attentive, sometimes less so—always returning in the same way and starting over. More often, I was beckoned by a cry. A bedtime story. A demand for milk. Some things, I soon learned, could wait and, given enough time, could become something else. That spring I learned to plant something other than grass. Alongside my son, a toddling boy-god, I blew dandelions and watched as seeds flew off in a hush, as if they were carrying a secret.

CURRENT

And you are ever again the wave
sweeping through all things.
    —Rilke (II.3)

In a single gust, it seems,
the leaves yellow
and one evening, I find the maple bare,
the last of summer burnished.
The trees know no vanity.
I walk around a manmade lake
and tell my son
that the birch kept growing
just to meet him.
Pay attention, the boughs sigh.
It is against trees that I measure
the dawning of his life
as an arc of a single ring.

An ocean over,
a mulberry tree stands in the same spot
as it did twelve hundred years ago,
for the most part ignored
until everything around it was replaced
with stones and gods,
and someone ran a hand over its surface,
recognized patience, vast and slow.

Somewhere, as it's done each fall,
a moose rubs its antlers among the trees,
branch against branch.

My son wonders up
at the new starkness of the maple,
the exposed scaffolding of autumn.
You lift a fallen prong of bones
and begin to work,
naming and renaming
each leafless thing.

WASAGA

We drive past strawberry and raspberry farms on our way to Wasaga Beach. Wasaga Beach, the water a mantle of blue. Blue waves bring shells and seagull feathers. Feathers cling to the rocks where the baby plays. Playing the sunbeams at the edge of water, he stops to watch me. *Mama,* he calls me back to him. Him, puff brown legs, the smallest feet in the water. The water ripples towards me even beneath his careful steps, distant and testing the waves as he walks in. In my arms he shivers, but there is raspberry staining his mouth and sand everywhere. Sand everywhere beneath the sun as we dry: in our hair, in the creases of our clothes, and the winter white folds of his chin.

BABBLE

A speck—a gravity—hauled out from sea,
shapes no words, dissolves to sound.
It twirls its hair in its sleep.

Every day it swivels to speak
and tests the banks of volume's bounds.
A speck—a gravity—made of the sea.

We commune in *kloos* and *mmms* and *hees*
until purled eve comes round.
It twirls its hair in its sleep.

With each utterance, I recede;
my glossary loses ground.
A speck—a gravity—mislays the sea.

Break my heart (in two or three)
in words that silt up, astound.
For now, it twirls its hair in its sleep.

It's too late; there's no release.
Already this script is mispronounced.
A speck of sea twirls his hair
and sleeps and dreams of gravity.

SITTING INSIDE THE MOON

After giving birth, it is customary in Chinese culture for a woman to spend one month housebound in order to recover from the rigours of labour. She does not shower, wash her hair, do chores, or touch cold water. She adheres to a strict diet, typically prepared by her own mother. She is permitted only to rest in bed and breastfeed.

Some have described this month-long refuge as "postnatal confinement." Such a translation makes it seem that the beginning of motherhood is a kind of imprisonment, which some would say it is. A new mother finds herself abiding the schedule of the newborn, held captive by their needs. Their needs, admittedly basic—hunger and sleep—are chased in a seemingly endless and clamorous rotation.

A more accurate translation of this Chinese practice, 坐月子 *(zuò yuè zi)*, is "sitting the month." The mother, in her state of rest and restricted activity, sits the month away. The character *"yuè"* also means "moon." A month, true to the lunar calendar, spans the time from one new moon to the next. To sit the month is to sit |on| the moon.

In my dialect, Hokkien, this practice goes by another term that translates to "within (or inside) the month." My preferred understanding of this hazy newborn period is that the mother is, more accurately, "sitting inside the moon." Perhaps there is no better analogy for the immediate cocooning and circling we do around a young life, like a satellite. We tend to their cries, pacing with them in our arms around a room. It is a state that is marked not only by the celestial communion of soothing and nursing a newborn at all times in the night, but also the sheer lunacy of those early days: fear, doubt, exhaustion, and astonishment.

★

My water broke in the morning on the last day of May, minutes after I woke up. Afterward, I took out the recycling. I cleaned the bathroom. I emptied the dishwasher. From time to time, I would sit in the bathtub, naked from the waist down. The calmness of the morning lasted a short hour before I found myself white-knuckled in the tub, muttering, *This is only going to get worse.* The thought was followed by the fear that I had carried with me in the last weeks: the realization that once labour started, there was absolutely nothing that could halt or postpone it.

I was as prepared as anyone who had never given birth could be. I clung to the words of the doula in the prenatal class who told us to trust our bodies, that we would produce endorphins as labour intensified, that there were measures already put in place. *It doesn't just go from zero to a hundred,* she had said. I recalled the instructor from the other prenatal workshop who described the contractions as waves crashing, and then demonstrated the right sound to make in order to ride each wave safely to shore. It was a low creaturely moan emerging from deep in her stomach, and it filled the room with startling crescendo. We laughed, embarrassed, and then she assured the circle of pregnant women, *Guaranteed, when the time comes, each one of you will moo like a cow. Think of me when you do.*

★

There are no words in that incalculable period of time when a woman's body decides to set free the small life that was harboured intimately within her own. Just as the newborn does not immediately penetrate the barrier of speech, a woman reverts to a similar state of infancy where there are no words accessible, meaningful, accurate, or explicit enough. Words, as most have or will experience, always fall short in moments of tremendous love, grief, and pain—but in labour there is a speechlessness that transforms the mouth into pure animal drive. My mouth, usually a vehicle for coherent expression, was humbled; I suddenly found my body taking precedence, and where it went in those hours there were no words.

When the contractions come, don't resist. Don't fight it. Invite them in. Let your body do the work. Let go. These phrases, despite the videos I was shown and the conversations I had with other mothers, floated in the air and never caught onto anything resembling comprehension. They were words that told me nothing until after the fact, when I realized that to let go was to let go of words and whatever life those words contained. It was, in a way, to let go of my own life and any control I had over it. To surrender is to give up, to deliver over. I knew that to surrender my body was to give it over to the surges of intensity, discomfort, and unknowable pressures that were part of giving myself over to another human. I disappeared. What the body does in the emergence of new life is a process that cannot be measured sensibly by time or language. Between my water breaking and my son being placed on my chest, eight hours passed. And yet there is nothing that I can recall that had the pace or venture of a typical nine-to-five day.

To be with child is to possess delight. In Chinese, the characters 有喜 *(yǒuxǐ)*, which means "pregnant," or "expecting," is to literally "have happiness" in one's body. That morning, it seemed incongruous that in order to express that happiness in the form of a child, one would have to endure an ordeal such as labour. In the midst of that dark loss, I felt that I was surely progressing to some nameless void. I saw, in those flitting moments when I opened my eyes, that there was an end and it could not possibly be good. The only words I recall uttering as I strained at sense were, *This baby is killing me.* My husband, upon hearing that, was stunned into understanding as my belly tremored and tightened from some invisible hand. He, in turn, had no words.

If all goes well, the baby will make it out alive, and so will you. Nonetheless, you will have touched death along the way, says Maggie Nelson.[11] Before I found my way to that void, my body was ready to push. I had been ebbing out, further from the strata of words, but then I heard voices calling me back. I don't know what to call the void, if it was what Nelson terms death. *This must be what it feels like to die,* I blurted between contractions. And there was death in that room when my son finally surfaced from that place where neither one of us could speak. The extinguishing of who I was before. I, new, surfaced alongside him, and when I began to bleed after his emergence, when the team of nurses worked quickly to stop the hemorrhaging and he was wet and asleep against me, I heard voices through the dizzying end: *Look at your baby. Look at your baby.*

It is said that when a baby exits the mother's body, what is left is empty space. During the sitting of the month, women must rid themselves of this air where once the baby resided. In order to do so, their diets are restricted to foods categorized as "hot." Hot foods, according to the Chinese, include chestnuts, onions, chicken, ginger, vinegar, cloves. Just as there are hot foods, there are also "cold" foods. These include pomelo, bamboo shoots, lotus roots, duck eggs, and chrysanthemum.

The warming and cooling characteristics of food have been used by Chinese medicine practitioners to balance the energies of the body. If one's body is "hot," which includes states such as thirst, perspiration, anxiety, having headaches or vivid dreams, then cooling foods can counteract and quell the heat. If one's body is "cool," such as experiencing cold extremities, stomach pains, bloating, and sore joints, hot foods raise the energy, or *qi*, of the body, thus dispelling the cold. A postpartum body, too, requires careful recalibrating.

Postpartum diets vary from village to village and province to province. Living in Hong Kong, my aunt followed the Cantonese tradition in which the main dish is pork feet (specifically the back trotters) stewed in sweetened vinegar, ginger, and an array of Chinese herbs. The dish is valued for the collagen from the tendons which, when consumed, encourages the uterus to quickly shrink back to its original state.

While traditionally baths or showers are not allowed for fear that the mother would catch a chill, my aunt was permitted ginger baths. Ginger, a staple ingredient in postpartum care, is said to increase milk production, ease the discomfort of colic, and improve the flow of *qi*. To prepare the bath, ginger skin is laid out, dried, and then boiled. The water, acquiring the root's hot properties, is then suitable to receive the newly maternal body.

In the months before my son was born, my mother prepared for my recovery by finely chopping up ginger root after ginger root and frying them until they were black. She then packed jars of darkened minced ginger away in her freezer until the fateful day when I would add a pungent spoonful to everything I ate.

For breakfast, she would serve me fermented rice simmered in a lightly sugared soup along with sweet rice balls and a poached egg. To make fermented rice, my mother would add a particular yeast to cooked rice, wrap the closed bowl in a towel, and find a warm spot in the home for it to effervesce. The bowl found a place in our bedroom near the west-facing window where it sat for a week. The longer it was allowed to ferment, the sweeter it would be. The alcohol in the rice, considered hot, would encourage blood circulation. A couple of weeks after giving birth, I was also permitted a shot glass of rice wine with my dinner.

My mother's efforts to restore strength to my body extended beyond dietary restrictions. She prohibited me from standing in front of open doors or windows where a draft could steal in and find me. I was to stay bundled despite the summer heat. While my mother would go out and garden, I would hold my son and watch from behind a pane, my insides burning from the ginger laced into my lunch. She had brought with her a small rose cutting from my grandmother's rose bush that she transplanted to an empty plot in the front yard. I watched her hands deep in the soil, her shoulders warmed from the sun. When she returned inside, I told her I was envious, and she showed me the mosquito bites on her arms as consolation.

It didn't take me long to become listless and, in the middle of the month, when she cut some peonies from the yard and brought them in, it was hard not to see this as a gesture of generosity, or mercy.

★

To sit inside the moon is to exist apart from everyone else. A day does not keep the same hours. It is a time marked instead by rhythms: cries, hunger, spontaneous interpretation, perceivable and minute changes, one's own weeping. At one week old, I noticed that my son's skin was starting to peel. He was a small animal moulting. In my joy and delirium at his growth, I cried and said, *You almost never meet someone you've made.* When I nursed him at night, I would watch the moon at the left edge of the window. By the time he was done and asleep again, the moon had moved to the right.

The time one sits inside the moon is so particular, so isolated from real time and the real world, that if a new mother were to become ill, the only time she could heal would be during the next moon-sitting. She would, in short, have to have another baby. The body of the mother would retain a kind of moon memory.

The cautionary tale that was told to the women in my family involved my grandmother. My grandfather had returned home from a business trip with a cold. My grandmother had recently given birth to my aunt, her third child. It was said that my grandmother was already weak from staying up nights with my aunt, who was a sickly and inconsolable infant. When my grandmother caught my grandfather's cold, she developed asthma. The village doctor who examined her diagnosed the asthma as being particular to the month-long sit. He informed her that any sickness developed in this time would have to be treated similarly. She had to sit inside the moon again, trouble-free, and, if successful, her health would be restored.

My aunt was seven months old when my grandmother became pregnant again. Those who were there for that birth said that because she was treating her asthma during the pregnancy, the child emerged so healthy that even her hair stood up strong and at attention. Despite her asthma improving, my grandmother was still not completely recovered. And so another baby was born two years later. And then another. By then, her asthma disappeared and, to this day, has never returned.

To sit inside the moon is to be aware of spaces. To feel the empty quiet of the shrivelling belly. To be aware that the home accommodates another life. To learn again how to be a person—to be a new person—in the space of the moon and, eventually, the world beyond. I found the perfect opposition between the words "surrender" and "recover" after my son was born. If to surrender is to give something over, then to recover is to get something back. There is a return, but it is hard to say who or what exactly comes back.

The Chinese purport to get rid of empty space inside the mother's body via diet, rituals, and restrictions, but what does it mean to encounter and eliminate this space? It is impossible to ignore the first dwelling of a baby. Once the cord is severed, a mother must acknowledge that the child took up vacancy in a space once belonging only to her. Suddenly that space has taken form as a being with observable eyes, a chin, elbows, fingertips, soft bones. When I looked at my son for the first time, I was in awe that he had features. I had been staring at the bland topography of my belly for so long that it didn't occur to me that the child could be as complex as he was. I saw then that he made his way, moon-side, to sit with me. I understood that he was no longer only mine, sheathed beneath my skin, but out here, looking like everybody else.

Sitting inside that moon gave me time to begin the process of recovery. Not only a return to health but to have something else come back to me. Language slowly returned. I suddenly spoke to the baby in Hokkien, remembering words from an earlier time, phrases that I had never used on anybody else. I learned new language. I learned to distinguish the severity of his cries, the crooning sounds, the rooting mouth after a nap. In my sleep-sapped state, I found myself forgetting language and used the simplest or crudest words to express how I was feeling. At one point, three weeks in, I was overwhelmed and frustrated by the insistence of my son's hunger that when I pulled him close to my breast, I called him a jerk. The word hung between us in the dark in the middle of the night. Guilty, I added, *You're lucky you're cute.*

But recovery wasn't about getting myself back. I realized, with each passing day in the moon, that a return to a prior version was impossible. It would only be a semblance of recovery. It wasn't just the body (which many know firsthand preserves the marks of motherhood), but the self. There was, in truth, no old self to return to. In that startling all-consuming maternal love, in that other-worldly time when I was sheltered with a small stranger, I was also piecing a new self together. Some parts were recognizable and familiar. Many parts were not. Everything slowly took up space.

★

Part of sitting inside the moon is not reading. My grandmother laughed when I asked why. The answer was obvious: girls didn't learn to read back then. Nowadays, it is discouraged to read because a new mother has to protect her eyes. I had to make sure not to strain a single part of my body. It was an adjustment not to be able to read. It had been something I had done every day of my life since I could remember. The written word was prohibited. I had to learn to be in a world with my son with only the words I already had, and the new language I had to learn.

Writing was one of the first things to leave me. For a long time, even after I was done sitting in the moon, this part of me stayed quiet, returning only surprisingly and sporadically. A villanelle when my son was three months old. Another poem a few months later. I wrote at a rate of a poem per season, the tasks of writing and mothering always in conflict: one demanding time, space, and silence, the other impossibly stingy with all of those. *The writing will come back,* a friend, who was also both a mother and a poet, assured me. *Life is large,* another said.

But I found a limit to words in that first month. It was as solid as the door my mother would forbid me from opening, or the windows that stayed shut. *The limits of my language mean the limits of my world.*[12] The limits of my infant mean the limits of my world.

Louise Glück writes that we are only poets when we are writing poetry. To be a poet is an aspiration, not an occupation. So when I am not writing a poem, I am someone who just *wants* to be a poet.[13] I spent time with my son astonished at how efficiently motherhood replaced this act of writing. Writing was supplanted by other functions: nursing, consoling, rocking, diaper-changing, dressing, burping, gazing. I was tethered to the baby by an imaginary and taut thread and I circled through these acts, one after the other. If writing was not taking place, then the poet in me, according to Glück, diminished to a mere potential. This thought created anxiety. I was accustomed to the freedom, space, and leisurely pace of enactment. The quiet was swiftly broken.

I feared for a while that I had lost language on the day my son was born. I was afraid that I returned to shore leaving words behind and irrecoverable. My language, like my body, was imbalanced and weak. But I discovered in early motherhood that what

I thought was loss was more like rest. I was resting from poetry. *Poems are not, as people think, simply feelings . . . they are experiences,* writes Rilke.[14] My rest from words allowed me to be a collector of all-consuming and ceaseless experiences that a newborn could demand and offer. I ventured into a space in which words couldn't keep up. The rapidity of a baby's growth and development in the first months was evidenced by clothes that were barely worn, boxed, and stored away. The emergence of a smile that was willed and not reflexive, as it is in those early days when a newborn smiles by accident, renewed life as I knew it.

I would learn, in the months to come, that both acts of nurturing and writing were equally acts of love. They were days of attention. My son, for a while, would be preoccupied with his hands, particularly the right one. He would hold his right arm straight out in front of him and study his fingers. In the mornings, he would smile upon waking. I would peer over his bassinet to see an unworldly happiness fill his body with twists, bucks, and kicks. He would find me staring and laugh. Sometimes I was vain enough to think that I was the sole cause of this delight, but it soon became clear that it emanated only from him: a rapt triumph caused by his being alive, seeing another morning, and simply being in the prismatic world.

My pen could only fall behind. I learned that while the writing itself is valuable, it was not the only thing. As Rilke noted, to my relief, it was also the experiencing and the experimenting. The sleepy, broken, and incoherent notes I took as I tried to be a mother, and tried to be a writer at the same time.

Sitting in the moon is a transformation. You come out of it no longer the same person and no longer the same poet.

★

My mother continued to garden that summer. She grew petunias, geraniums, and impatiens. She would pluck phlox from neighbouring homes and set them in our soil. Across the street, someone offered her a single hosta plant from their garden.

When will this end? I asked myself one night when I heard my son's cries, just mere hours after setting him down. By morning, I roused to love. In the last week of the month, I observed his eyes grow alert and begin to follow voices and faces. Everything about him was less wrinkly. I counted down the days until I could go outside. I saw one morning how he had outgrown me: when he was curled against my body, his head almost reached my chin. I imagined how if he were to be put back inside of me, he wouldn't fit.

On the day that I could finally go outside, I stepped out and ate ice cream with lemon meringue pie in the sun. My son, beside me, kicked his feet with such force that his socks slipped off. My mother joined me later and observed the flowers adorning the home. As usual, she crouched down to pluck a few weeds. I stared into and got lost in the deep flush of the peonies. I worried about the blur of the past month and hoped that in my preamble into motherhood, I had done it "right," whatever that meant. Suddenly, beyond the moon, I worried if and how my exhaustion and re-creation marked him unfavourably. Before I turned to go back inside, carrying the small body of my son, alive and squirming in the summer air, my mother glanced down at the flowerbed and called out to me. *The roses,* she said, *are thriving.*

QUEEN MARY ROAD

veined and clamped to the season

the city is asleep on her back
upturned breast
there is no way to turn from
the exposure
unflinching beneath fog

the light slips along the oratory's dome
milky and sore-quarried

a trace of the baby's cry
left meandering through the night

as I retreat into the sun
and down the pappled road

where the shadow of my worn bosom
unmissable
takes shape

KINDLING

And after days of rain, it suddenly stops and we peer out the window, watch the grey lift. Across the street, someone from the city has set up around an old stump. The grinder whirrs away as chips spit out, amass into a velvet pile. My son, who has learned to climb, clambers onto a stool and plays the radiator like a piano. On tiptoes he regards the man in goggles, the slow work of shredding years and smoothing out land. Damp grass encircles an open wound. When he was just learning to crawl, my son and I sat on the kitchen floor counting knots in the wood. Now it's just the two of us, each on two feet; one startled by how swift and brute the uprooting, another contemplating how to fly.

ARCHAEOLOGY

If it weren't for the onesies and sleepers
classified in old diaper boxes
and passed down to exhibit
in other family photos or holiday cards—
who would remember?

It's not just the pair of baby socks
forgotten in a winter pocket
or a burp cloth clinging to the sheets.
There are also the baby spoons
cluttered at the back of the drawer,
the ones I, just today, extracted
from that dark otherside and collected
into a petrified bundle.

Fluorescent tools
once aimed at the gaping portals
of some prehistoric fish—

with these small shovels
I believe, for a moment, I can expose
the ancient clade,
perch on that branch of existence
before you inched ashore

the looming child;
a mouth full of teeth.

CAPRICORN ONWARDS

Crows caw their way through the quiet.
The coast is snowed on, slushed, frozen over.
I watch a man crouch, take a cleaver to the ice.
A car froths at its wheels, a heavy foot squeals frustrated.
A gull perches and peruses the scene.
Someone dies, someone dies, someone dies.
Smoke from the neighbouring low-rise swells silent.
A black squirrel leaps from the balcony
to the moss-fringed maple: bracket to branch.
Fog against cloud, the sky whispers to the birds arcing,
Where do you go when I look away?

THE HESITANT GAZE
Some Notes on Looking

To be painted by Cézanne was a nightmare.

He was known not only as a bad-tempered man, but also a slow painter. There could be over one hundred separate sittings for Cézanne to complete a single portrait and, even then, he would instruct his subject to sit *like an apple.*[15]

By contrast, the modern selfie takes mere seconds to capture. In comparison to the diligent eye of the portrait painter, the lens of a smartphone pays only the briefest of attention. (The result, to the relief of many, is transient: it is editable, filterable, trashable, retakeable.) I began to wonder: how long do we spend looking at an object? What emerges from long looking?

When I imagine being painted by Cézanne, I realize that the challenge is not to be motionless like resting fruit, but to be caught and pressed under the artist's unnerving gaze. The difficulty is to be scrutinized, construed or misconstrued, and then extracted onto canvas.

In ekphrastic poetry, poets engage with a painting, sculpture, drawing, or other visual object from which the poem will derive. What does it mean to look? To focus a gaze that is sustained, interrogative, receptive, challenging, and vulnerable? The stark intimacy of a look can stop the viewer in their steps, as Jeanette Winterson once experienced when seeing a painting in Amsterdam: "What was I to do, standing hesitant, my heart flooded away?"[16] Ekphrasis is not only to compose a text inspired by the artwork itself, but also to be carried off by the uncontainable surge of memory and affect, judgment and speculation. It is to dive under, eyes first.

★

A survey found that an average museum visitor would spend seventeen seconds looking at a painting.[17] Another survey found that visitors spent less than thirty seconds and rarely more than two minutes.[18] According to a more recent study, the mean time spent looking at a work was 28.63 seconds.[19] For someone like Da Vinci, who continued to work on (and look at) the *Mona Lisa* until his death, these numbers are no doubt disappointing.

Pen in hand, I wanted, as Winterson did, to give an artwork my full attention. Before composing the ekphrastic poem, I chose to look at a given artwork for exactly one hour. All the while I would free-write, allowing my look to deepen so what I saw plunged from general observations to woven narratives, invented possibilities, fantasies, anxieties, and personal memory. The longer I paid attention, the more I saw: brush strokes, dripped paint spots, and the seductive texture of canvas. I realized that while my looking was stuck in our own linear time, I could also create time in my own medium. A painting captures one moment. A look, a hand raised up to a mouth, a sitting apple—these things were fixed, trapped within a frame by the artist. But in poetry, I could fold, replay, imagine, and extend the lines of time and movement any which way. Paintings, I noticed, wanted me to be involved. To write from what I saw was to write what I would eventually allow readers to see of myself. My gaze wandered and knocked along intimate bends.

John Berger tells us that "we never look at just one thing; we are always looking at the relation between things and ourselves."[20] Similarly, Winterson describes an exchange of emotion that arises from long looking that takes place between the artist, the painting, and the viewer.[21] (Ekphrasis anticipates an exchange with an anonymous fourth: the reader of the poem who is always to come.) This exchange, or *conversation*, as I saw it, was always different. The permanent collection at the local fine arts museum, free to the public at the time, allowed me to look at a piece as many times as I wanted. My frequent visits quickly revealed the changes in the relation felt between the work and myself. While I believed I controlled the process (I chose the painting I would write on after all), I was surprised to discover that *I* was the variable in the experiment.

Looking had a Heraclitan effect. Time was the river I couldn't step in twice. Time would pass, life would change as it did, and, suddenly, the poem I envisaged when I first saw a painting became impossible to write by the next visit. Sometimes the falseness of the first poem came through. In that case, the poem had to be scrapped because of a bewildered subsequent look that felt truer—at times more difficult—than the first.

★

I encountered John Lyman's painting, *The Artist's Father* (1922), for the first time at Montreal's Musée des beaux-arts. I was completing my master's thesis, a collection of ekphrastic poetry, which would eventually be published as *Fish Bones*. At that point in 2008, I had returned to Winnipeg only twice in four years since leaving for university to pursue a degree in literature and creative writing. The silence between my father and me had extended much longer.

When I first looked at Lyman's painting, I was stunned by empathy. The father figure sits on a mustard yellow armchair, dressed in suit and tie, and holds a book open. His attention is directed only at the page in front of him. I recognized the father's deliberate position as one of formal indifference. The bones of his elbow and knees are aimed away from the viewer. The lens of his glasses point downwards so any possibility of a returned gaze is blocked by black rims. I looked into the picture and felt nobody look back at me.

When engaging in the ekphrastic mode, freewriting allowed me to pluck and pull close words, thoughts, and events that floated both within and without me. Some details zipped past, taunting, at times registered and put into words, at times escaping. Reading over my scrawls, I noted the number of times I recorded conversations taking place around me, or mentioned the echo of shoes across the gallery floor, the glowing red EXIT sign, or my admission of hunger or boredom. Of course, these never made it into the final poem but, however tangential, they were part of that hour of attentiveness.

Over the years, I've described my ekphrastic writing using a number of analogies. A painting typically took on the role of a catalyst, a springboard, the opening notes, the wave of the wand. I was the viewer and the poet, but I was also the chemist, the gymnast, the conductor, and the magician. Lyman's painting offered an unexpected experience. I stood in front of it, whole-bodied, with a sense of trespass. I was, in short, provoked. Art is an upheaval. Paint can make one suddenly sad.

My first response to *The Artist's Father* is one that embarrasses me now. It carries in its lines the angst and rigidity of adolescence, a simplifying of emotion, the arrogant edges of rage. To look at Lyman's painting was to return to childhood, to Winnipeg, and to my father's resolute skepticism. I left home and *didn't look back*, as they say, but visual art forced me to look, to revisit and, eventually, to re-examine.

I advise my students to take time between the drafts of their poems. I say that it is important to gain some emotional and temporal distance from their work so that both their lived experiences and literary encounters can accumulate, however intentionally or arbitrarily. Given enough time, the right accidents can take place for the writer to *become* the writer that the poem needs. The poet returns to the work with the clarity and heft that were once missing and that the draft rightfully deserves. And just as we become the reader that we couldn't foresee, we also become a new viewer, one who steps into the painting like a portal, carrying with us something different each time.

Between my first look at Lyman's painting and my second, I was visited by a ghost. It was a necessary visit. My father's father—a man who passed away before I was born—stepped into my world, by chance, during a phone call with my uncle. From my uncle I learned that my grandfather wasn't dead, which was what I had always been led to believe. Instead, he had actually disappeared from my father as a child and was alive somewhere in Ontario. I realized then the ambiguity with which my father had always described my grandfather. I remembered my father pulling out an old album full of stamps, a collection of souvenirs that proved a correspondence, a relationship. I would never see the letters. When asked about my grandfather's absence, my father would skirt my questions and barely nod at my words. He neither denied nor confirmed anything, just gently adjusted a loose stamp into place.

I don't know why my uncle chose that phone call to tell me that their father didn't just trip and fall deathward in some unlucky accident, leaving my grandmother alone to raise three sons. Perhaps enough time had passed. Perhaps too much. But when my uncle's words settled around me, I looked backwards in a new way. I turned west and the lines softened.

I returned to the museum and could no longer look at Lyman's painting from that previous vantage point. So many facets of my looking had changed and my poem followed. When I saw Lyman's father again, still sitting there reading just as I had left him, I glimpsed an ache that I would never have noticed before.

After I completed my M.A. and finally received my thesis, professionally bound in red with my name on the cover in gold, I visited Winnipeg and hand-delivered an inscribed copy to my father. It was a creative thesis consisting of the ekphrastic poems I had written. It contained hours of looking. I never expected enthusiasm from him—he who never wanted me to leave Winnipeg in the first place—but I recognized some growing acquiescence to my studying literature. My move to Montreal was made only increasingly acceptable as my schooling advanced. I was hopeful that upon presentation of the thesis, a tangible outcome of my leaving and an achievement that even I never envisioned, we could turn a corner. It was my way of saying, "Look!"

The book was newly bound and its spine was stiff. The short lines of my verse reached, at most, only halfway across the page. The pages themselves were woven tight. After my father took the book, examined both front and back covers, and tested its weight, he thumbed through the pages and exclaimed, aghast at the blank spaces surrounding the poetry, "There's nothing here—it's empty!"

When I first started teaching, my father, the analytical engineer, asked me how many Chinese colleagues I had. (This was a version of a game that I was accustomed to playing, especially when I was one of the very few Asian students enrolled in the creative writing program.) Always interested in numbers, my father then asked how many Chinese students I had. Then he asked me what it was like when my students looked at me standing there, taking up space at the front of the class.

"Are your students surprised that you don't have an accent?"

By then I was in a place of some stability and self-confidence with regards to my writing. I had published, I was completing a Ph.D., and, more importantly, I had slowly surrounded myself with a small supportive community of creators and friends. His question exposed a fault line. When I replied, "What kind of accent would I have? A western Canadian one?" he sort of grunted at my briskness and didn't elaborate. We both knew what he meant, as absurd as I first thought. And still his question remains. At the start of classes, I take my place at the front, face the expectant stare of new students, open my mouth, and wonder.

★

The poetry that followed my first book clarified my process of looking. A long-time reader of William Carlos Williams, I was moved by his visions of particularity, resonance, and everyday simplicity. I witnessed in his poems a *hesitation*, as the poet paused at the sight of a leg, the taste of cold plums, a red wheelbarrow. I, too, wanted to write with hesitance. I wanted poetry that lingered on the image, powerful and incandescent. The poet's hesitation, as I understand it, is that slow, careful deliberation that sets the reader aglow.

When I arrived in Fujian, the land of my parents—all dream and whisper and story—I recalled the words of Winterson, who considered long looking at art as equivalent to "being dropped into a foreign city, where gradually, out of desire and despair, a few key words, then a little syntax make a clearing in the silence."[22] I regarded my encounter with cultural difference and deep family history as I regarded a painting. At first I was uncertain if I could feel such an inquisitive distance when surrounded by extended family and crowds of people who, for the first time, all looked like me. But alienation came quickly. Wherever I was, locals would look at me and know at once—perhaps it was my shoes or my gait—that I was, what they freely called an outsider. They would test out Cantonese on me. Failing that, Mandarin. Failing that, I would suggest the local dialect, Hokkien, and they would shake their heads, acknowledging themselves as someone from outside Fujian.

Language was tangled, lost, and recovered on the other side of the world. My parents would jump from dialect to dialect. I would be comforted by their voices but was often slow to keep up with surrounding conversations. By and by, immersion jogged my memory and years of Saturday Chinese school suddenly poked through with success. I found myself reading characters written on road signs and storefronts. I seized what I could.

It was only abroad that I realized how questions about language came from all sides. In Canada, I grew up accustomed to people swinging their eyes from my parents to me and asking if I spoke English. But here I was, far from my place of birth, closer to the history of my parents, and yet, to my surprise, detectible to the practiced eyes of the locals who asked if I spoke Chinese. I became used to finishing each day alone with a notebook, furiously recording and composing. Those moments were necessary. Out of desire, maybe out of frustration, I turned to poetry in a way I hadn't before: a way of coming up with a language that could be unquestionably my own.

I found myself one summer collaborating on a short film with friend and filmmaker Sofia Bohdanowicz. We adapted my poem "Arriving," written about my visit to my father's childhood home in Fujian. The past, as Sofia described it, was tactile: in my poem she saw the movement of people, the passage through generations, my father's return, my missing grandfather, and my visit as things that could be felt by the hands. The gaze had texture. In order to achieve this haptic looking, we rented a Bolex camera for $10 a day, and shot on 16 mm film.

The film we used was bought on eBay and had been expired for nearly thirty years. Our process, much to my delight, was driven by risk and unknowability. Using expired film meant that there was a possibility it would not develop correctly and we would end up just having reams of black. I learned that there was even a compensatory calculus: for every decade it was expired, the aperture had to be opened up wider a certain degree to make up for its age. It also turned out that the film we bought, which was discontinued in 1989, wasn't a light-sensitive stock to begin with, which made it difficult to expose.

It was precisely this sense of chance that would determine our looking and our mechanics of capture. What was it like to hesitate and stick fast to memory? Story? Film? What could be created as we worked through these imperfections, variables, and mistakes? How was this looking through the lens so much like all of the looking I had experienced? In all of its familiarity as well as its surprise, misconception, and revision?

Before we began shooting, Sofia took the cans of film, which contained 400-feet of film each, and spooled them down to 100-foot spools in order to fit the Bolex. All of this had to be done in the darkroom. She used her hands to see in the dark, at one point accidentally spooling the film backwards, and having to unspool and do it all over again. I thought of this when later we filmed my hands flipping through my father's stamp album. I ran my palms over the plastic protective sheets, searching.

★

The Bolex was first manufactured in the 1930s. It weighs about five and a half pounds and is manually run. Inside is a spring motor designed to be wound by a crank. In order to film, one has to turn the winding crank counter-clockwise. Once fully wound, the motor drives about eighteen feet of film through the camera. This amounts to about twenty-eight seconds. When filming, the long looking I was used to was replaced by selective looking, a process that made us self-conscious and careful. There was only so much time to capture. There were also only so many spools of film, only so much budget, and so much daylight.

Sofia and I spent our days chasing light. We would wake early to take advantage of the sun, filming what we could all the while uncertain but hopeful that the images would take. On our last day of shooting, as the afternoon began to fade, we decided to equip ourselves with more light. We bought portable halogen work lights and set them up near the kitchen table where we filmed my hands wrapping wontons. The lights had to be bright enough, so we turned them on full blast. By the end of the shoot, they were so hot that they had started to melt the stands. We pushed time when we created light. And there were so many temporal threads to consider: the time in the poem, the time afforded by the Bolex, the time of the shooting, the time we edited out, the time we kept, and the final time of the film. All the while, Sofia and I were in the time of art, where we felt precisely the phenomena described by Winterson about looking at a painting: "a constant exchange of emotion" between us, the poem, and the film.

The experience of working with Sofia and the materials of film gave me a new and clearer understanding of my own medium. For Robert Beavers, an experimentalist filmmaker who worked with the Bolex: "The shutter in the camera is like the wings of an insect. Both create movement, one in space, the other in the eye."[23] The poet too is the curtain flicked aside to let through the light. I try to hold myself open long enough so that it may confront and impress itself upon some black obscurity.

As for our film, we were relieved to discover, after Sofia returned to Toronto and developed the reams, that the images took. Our hours of arranging, looking, winding, and light-chasing were edited and produced into an eight-minute short film.[24] When it was done, we let the art object into the world, unsure how it would be received, but hopeful it would encounter—in our absence and however briefly—the infinitesimal, ephemeral flash of recognition.

ABOVE, THE GEESE

Watch as winter's footman scurries off,

the winged spring melt rushing beneath long plates of ice.

Look at the water

pregnant with twigs and lost coins.

Where the trunk meets the ground—

this snow is the first to go.

A tree carries its warmth through the winter,

each one a *point de capiton*

around which footprints stitch themselves.

For an instant—all is convinced

before moonlight kneels, as it does,

to cast each day away.

ON PROCESS

It's like this:
you have a basket of clean laundry—
mostly fresh clothes and a large tangled bedsheet.
The bedsheet is the first you take out to hang on the line.
The basket is bewitchingly light.
The bedsheet blows brightly
in the breeze.

ALL I HAVE TO SAY

There is a downy woodpecker that shows up from time to time behind my house. I admire him for his immaculate white and black feathers, the small spurt of red on his head. His pecking was so dulcet and unexpected when I first spotted him. But now I notice that his visits have started to wear away the crumbling lattice edging my deck. I've started to tap at the window to get him to fly off, but he keeps up his visits. He keeps pecking as a woodpecker does and makes his secret known to me with each strike: *Everything goes to oblivion. As it should.* He makes his noise. *And.* Peck. *That's.* Peck. *Good.* Peck. Nothing I do can stop him.

INAUGURATION
for E.

The week you were born, the ash tree in the yard met its last
    August.
Workers splintered it down from its impractical height.

The sound of the chipper buckled your cries, thin as you tested
    your reach,
startled by how I was suddenly beyond you.

Summer heat seeped into the house.

Beneath the porch, a black cat surrendered,
abandoning its last heat to the shadowed cool of foundation.

Logs piled up behind our shed, waiting for disposal.
The carcass was carted off.

And no, it wasn't easy then for you
to make the acquaintance of ceremony,

but when you squalled and I witnessed your tiny body
grow red and indignant in my arms, I was relieved—

each shriek, unsnarling the mysteries of your arrival.
Each wail, spurning everything as it fell.

THAT WORLD INVERTED

As I write this, I am awaiting the birth of my second child. This is a different experience from the birth of my son, who arrived unexpectedly in the drowsy morning, forcing our ambulance to cut in on a city-wide bicycle marathon. We plummeted into newness before any of us could protest or prepare. This time I am expectant, in all senses, and quietly impatient.

The body, as usual, remains inscrutable. A part of me is oblivious and believes that this is the same body, the one I have always had and known in adulthood, when in truth it is entirely different since my son's arrival three years ago. It is an animal-body, one that is looser, milk-producing, marked by the events of childbirth, achier, leakier, open. It harbours a memory of what it is to grow something monumental and unprecedented, to take what it needs, to work for a secret. It remembers what will come again in the culminating moment when life unfurls, distinct and shrieking. Late in my third trimester, I look down and see Plath's "ponderous house."[25]

It is also a body wrecked by sleeplessness.

When I was a university student, I could survive on little sleep. I worked at a coffee shop near campus where I usually opened. I managed to wake at 5:30 (a miracle I am now incapable of repeating), commute, and unlock the doors an hour later. After my shift, I would walk the few blocks to attend classes, leave campus in the late afternoon, fill my evenings however way I wanted, sleep at any hour, and do it all over again the next day. Exhaustion then was nearly laughable. Ingrained is the sensation of the bus lurching in the early mute hours of winter. I know that singular mood of winding downtown while a city sleeps, wondering at the cockcrow lives of other passengers who stumbled onboard.

But I loved to sleep. And on days I could, I would sleep straight into the afternoon. That gloriously slow waking into the silence of my room, undisturbed by alarm clocks and obligations.

Before my son was born, I was asked by a nurse if I planned to breastfeed. I said I would, all the while knowing very little about it. I had the now ludicrous idea that breastfeeding would occur three times a day, much like a regular eating schedule. After my son's wriggling mass was placed on my chest, the nurses instructed me that I would have to feed him every two to three hours around the clock. What I knew of sleep, a long dark ribbon, became perforated. Punctures in the night letting in only the light of stars and, at times, only more darkness.

I read that a new parent loses about six months of sleep in the first two years of a baby's life. In the velvet hours of the night when I was nursing or rocking a fussy baby, my mind drifted to the many hours I spent not sleeping when I should have, to the long stretches of sleep I achieved before children. I thought even as far back as the sleep I missed when I was a baby, or a resistant toddler. I shook my head at how, as a child, I thought staying up late was thrilling as I strayed into those unseen hours.

But now I, who was waking every two hours in the early months of my son's life (and barely any better until he was two), envied the black, tranquil squares of my neighbours' windows across the street. I envied the empty sidewalks. Even cars, completely at rest, nuzzled the curb and mocked my desire to drift off. I started reading up on the history of sleep deprivation as a torture method and questioned my son's innocence. My waking state at night felt like a malfunction as my body eventually gave way to chronic fatigue, headaches, and a constant state of blurriness. (*Or*, as a friend said lightly, *motherhood.*)

The usual period of repose certainly has its rebels: nightshift workers, taxi drivers, those on call, self-proclaimed night owls. There are also those who just can't get to sleep. But there is something awry about the unslept body as it crosses into dawn, still swaddled in night. In fact, the word "insomnia" in Chinese (失眠, shī mián) includes the verb 失 (shī), meaning "miss," "lose," or "fail." The same character also acts as a noun that means "mistake," or "mishap."

In Elizabeth Bishop's poem, "Insomnia," each line is edged with mistake, or, as she puts it, "that world inverted."[26] There is a sense of *wrongness* in staying up at night. In those early days of motherhood, I felt like the personified moon in her poem, "far and away beyond sleep," all the while tormented by the soft snores of my husband beside me, and a dozing newborn who found rest in my stiffening arms. It is no surprise that the moon can't seem to locate herself in Bishop's poem, as she is reduced to a mere echo and reflected in only a body of water, or the surface of a mirror.

While my nights were driven by maternal love—my son and I bound together through his hunger—Bishop's poem is one of unrequited love in which both the moon and the poet are weighed down by loneliness, yearning, and night. The distance between lover and beloved is comparable to that between sleep and wakefulness. The insomniac's desire spans the distance, which, in the final stanza, is marked by wrongness. All we know is "inverted": directions come unmoored, light deceives both shadow and body, the sky is stolen of its depth, and we are awake at night.

In the fog of those infant days, I found myself drawn to poems set in the middle of the night, moved by the voices of those who were also in a state of sleeplessness. I was curious about those who chose to stay up, and those who tried to sleep but couldn't. I wanted to know what ailed them and kept them awake. I was intrigued by how they existed when the rest of the world was far and rapt in slumber. Most of all, I wanted desperately to share the dark and my "failures" with somebody.

Loneliness in the middle of the night was also familiar to Sappho, whose fragment 168B is known as the "midnight poem."

Moon has set
and Pleiades: middle
night, the hour goes by,
alone I lie.[27]

The speaker observes the night sky, which functions as a marker of time. Once the moon and the constellation have disappeared from view, she drifts through the deepest centre of night, still awake. What I keep returning to in this bout of insomnia is the ending. How long after the hour goes by in the third line is the speaker still alone? Whom does she desire to join? And, more importantly, when will she at last fall asleep? The passing time in these lines may take up just an hour, but the frustration of lying alone in the dark always feels much longer In my own reading, time in this poem is the duration of the whole night, between midnight and the dreaded sunrise.

My own broken sleep kept me ensnared in those hours of black. In that time of sitting up with my son, I would overlap with those who passed my window. I thought of Amy Lowell, also up at 2 a.m., looking out onto her own street and seeing a cityscape that doesn't quite belong to her, nor her to it.[40] (An "alien city" she calls it.) The inhabitants of my night included the young couple pulling into their driveway after an evening out. The old man who dragged his cart behind him and rummaged through the shadowed recycling bins. Once, I spied my neighbour's daughter laugh and wave down to a boy who had slinked down from her window (at least, through my somnolence, I believe this was what I saw). Had I been asleep, I would have missed this balcony scene. Eventually, I would clash with those heading to work. Car doors echoing down the brightening street. The first sounds of an engine. Bleary-eyed, I followed their silhouettes under the fading streetlight.

★

In the first year of my son's life, I kept a record of our sleep. It was an ongoing list of times he roused, nursed, slept, and woke again throughout the night. It included his naps during the day, timed to the minute. I sought patterns, improvement, a progression towards longer, benevolent stretches of rest. At one doctor's appointment, overtired and overhopeful for answers, I showed her these pages. The doctor took one glance at the columns of numbers and said, "I don't understand what any of this is." I was baffled by everyone— other parents, doctors, child educators—who nodded in sympathy at the fragments of our sleep. While I could see that they were compassionate, they also seemed completely unperturbed. It felt like every other baby in the world was sleeping, and every new mother was faring beautifully.

During the day my mind felt slow and out of focus. I was thankful that I didn't own a car because I wouldn't have been able to operate it. At the first party I attended since giving birth, I carried my son the whole time. I didn't talk to anybody, stripped as I was of language, and drifting among all of those well-rested radiant-tongued beings. When my son was nearly two, some-one asked when I would go back to teach. I laughed in disbelief. *Imagine! Teaching like this!*

My own poems felt unreachable. I revisited Anne Sexton's "The Ambition Bird" and felt a bitter longing for her subject: "the busi-ness of words" and her box *full* of poems.[29] Shortly after becoming a mother, a friend had assured me that there would be days when I wouldn't feel like a good mother. Other days I wouldn't feel like a good writer or teacher. To accept that it is unfeasible to be good at everything on the same day is necessary to a new mother's survival. Something, as always, had to steal from somewhere. Something, somewhere, had to relinquish. My maternal lassitude forced its way to the front, elbowing past the luxury of creative exhaustion. Reading Sexton's poem as a mother, I found myself mapping her preoccupations over with my own. *So it has come to this [again] / ... the business of [my son] keeps me awake.*

★

Since starting this wandering and languid contemplation on sleep, I have given birth to my daughter. I have begun, once again, the pummelling sleep deprivation that I know all too well. I feel guilty about any hint of hesitation I experience when succumbing to the needs of my child while waving words away. Energy is diverted, inevitably and instinctually, to the present, the vulnerable, to those whose cries are for me alone. And yet words, though quieter, still turn in their beds.

What has kept us up? What calls to us throughout the night? Love. Poetry. The smallest child. Each insist on our attention, our un-rest. No matter how inconvenient, we cut out (or through) slumber to reply. I fumble now to the end of this piece, just as I feel through the dark towards the mewling baby. I want to finish this, not only as a personal ambition, but also so I no longer have to keep you up another night. What summons strings itself above me like unwavering stars. In my current state, when language is elusive, I think it best to borrow someone else's words.

There is a collection of Chinese songs that have been attributed to Zi Ye, a third-century poet. Whether her verses are written by an individual or a group of women remains unclear. Zi Ye is also known as "Lady Midnight." I stay up on this night to adjourn with her.

> The night is forever. I can't sleep.
> The clear moon is so bright, so bright.
> I almost think I hear a voice call me,
> and to the empty sky, I say *Yes?*[30]

FRICATIVES (A VISIT)

I am afraid to own a Body—
                    —Emily Dickinson

Through the window, spume-crested clouds.
From inside, I ride the sky,
settle into the usual loneliness of flying.

I read *The Letters of Emily Dickinson* to pass the time.
In May 1848, during her first year away at school,
Em wrote to say that she had not been well all winter
and refrained from telling her parents
lest the folks should take me home.

I float towards my parents
and take her with me.

★

Dawn stretches forward.
Beneath familiar sheets,
I sleep to the sounds of her slippered feet,
the scuff of heel against linoleum,
the precise silver clink of the kettle top.

A rustle.
The dried heads of chrysanthemums
bob and soften.

The day is a rubbing of another one.

Wear this jacket, she says, as he puts on his shoes.
A glance outside.
Or this one, she says, tugging it off a hanger.

★

My father tells me that the toughest vegetable to harvest
is the water chestnut.

They grow in ponds and are collected by hand
in the middle of winter.
The chill lends to the chestnut's sweetness.

Come spring,
you can plant the corms
and in eight months
when the culms yellow and die off from the first frost,
it's time to harvest once again.

He's dead, my mother says, matter-of-factly.
Outside it snows and the city, unprepared,
lies helpless beneath the slush clogging its streets,
keeps its cars spinning or stuck at their turns.

We are sitting at the kitchen table,
eating peanuts, cracking and disposing shells
onto old flyers.

Last month someone called, asking for my father.
I said he wasn't home. They told me to tell him.
Did you?
No.

The peanut shells pile up.

When Em's father died, she wrote to her cousins:
Father does not live with us now—he lives in a new house.
He hasn't any garden because he moved after gardens were made.

The snow here suddenly arrests the year.
Nothing sprouts, no wood is worked.
Nothing thaws.

Though it is many nights, Em continues,
my mind never comes home.
A father, too, may board a ship,
sail, and grow faint with the farthest ripple.

Tires squeal, vexed. Car doors slam.
Forget-me-nots and forsythias.

★

When I was small, my father told me
the secret to a long life:

In the days of winter, eat white radish.
In summer, eat ginger.

★

The two of us drive to Fraser and Forty-eighth
where the smell of roast duck wafts through the streets
and confuses the intersections.

Much younger, I whined to go home
and abandon the search for a chicken.
All the butchers said they were sold out
and good god, it's cold, can't we just go already?

My father stood at the corner,
the stiff wind ruffling back his hood,
and he said quietly, determined,
Please, can you give me more minutes?

This time we're close: there's a lineup at all the butchers
but the abundance of hanging birds looks promising.

I stare at their mute-plucked bodies through the glass
as he asks the woman, her fingers greasy,
about freshness, the price,
and yes, yes, include the head.

The cleaver quarters.
When I take the bag from her,
I remember how, one winter, Em
sent roasting chickens next door to her brother's family,
along with a note that read:
Brother, Sister, Ned.
Enclosed please find the Birds which do not go South.

★

Solstice dinner.
After the chicken's head is offered to ancestors,
after the men finish their tea in the living room,
after sweet rice flour is kneaded and rolled into small balls
between the hands of women,
after the leftovers are packed away
and the kitchen still hums of a place just used,

I spread out old newspaper,
open the tin box (too large for its contents:
a pair of scissors, a plastic comb, a folded stained apron)
and prepare to trim my mother's hair.

My grandmother assesses the fallen
and takes out the broom.
Between my fingers, my mother's hair is black enough
to overwhelm any peeks of grey.

We take turns in the chair,
barrettes and bobby pins
glimmering under stove light,

and though we are cheated of the day's hours,
we cut into the night,
circling each other as we let fall
and sweep up the ends.

★

My husband tells me, *You only get one.*

When he dreams of his father,
he grasps at sleep but details always slip out
through the hour's back door
and the morning has a way of coming in
before he can get a hold of it,
has a way of stopping breath, of saying,
Sorry, I have to.

For a while, my husband kept having the same dream
where his father, beaming,
tells him that his death was all a trick,
another joke to play on his mother.

When he woke,
he'd raise his head, looking confused but amused,
as if someone made a crack and he was the only one
who didn't get it. He'd look at me, vague-eyed, and ask,
Were you just laughing?

★

A little more of earnest, and a little less of jest,
Em once wrote in a letter to her brother.

My husband's favourite story about his parents
shows how a few words in a foreign language
can mask and moor the final lift of a question:

One dinner party, while still courting,
my father-in-law taught his soon-to-be-wife
a phrase she thought meant,

    Look, it's right over there.

In actuality, she uttered to a guest,

    Do you have eyes or the balls of a wasp?

Perfection and fluency, the earnestness in error.

I think of my father when even my computer
changes "I missyou" to "omissions."

And despite the better of his sixty years here,
when he begins a sentence with
To be honest with you,
it always sounds like
To belong to you.

★

My father moved through dooms of love.

The last apple of my grandmother's tree
hasn't fallen completely.
On its way down it lodged itself
in the nook of two branches,
and stuck there all fall, a foot above ground.

Now a shrivelled pulp, skin thin,
it collects snow, wears it like a nightcap,
and will sleep through the new year.

My mother and I grip onto my grandmother
as we make our way to the car.

My father moved through dooms of love.

He is motionless, sitting with the engine running.
We are slow, but the fall of the apple—
swift to its abrupt end.

The unit measure of love.
The lifespan of this December.

★

A cloud drops to its knees
at the side of the road
and the snow melts.

The panes stream
and the minutes slow
in the tawny light.

In the living room,
my grandmother, myopic,
sits too close to the television
as it murmurs
a Chinese soap opera.

After her program
she joins us in the kitchen for narcissus tea,
insists we stay seated as she slowly
makes her way to the counter,
lifts a hand for her mug.

My mother watches
while half-lifted off her chair
like a bird at a ledge,
a breath before takeoff.
My father turns the page
and then presses and clamps his hands together.
I know the damp makes them ache.

There is a word in Chinese
that means something between empathy
and sympathy.

Xinteng is a particular way
of feeling sadness and mutual pain,
but only for someone you love.

Pulled apart, the symbols *xin* (n. heart)
and *teng* (v. be fond of, adore; n. pain, or ache)
spring back to clasp you in a private embrace.

An exception:
did Em, who would observe funeral processions
from her bedroom window, feel *xinteng* for strangers?
She grew preoccupied by the services she could see
and became skilled at crafting letters of condolence.

The night before, my mother told me
how my grandmother had nothing left.
All jewels and jade were already divided, given
to her daughters, save for a wedding band
and her mother-in-law's crooked gold hairpins.

She said, *You can cry and cry*
and sleep
and feel your bones
come back together
in the morning,

and I recalled years that once stretched out
like a long, rolling highway,
remembering what looked like water up ahead
just recede and vanish as we drove closer.

Em wrote once,
I have thought of you often since the darkness,
—though we cannot assist another's night.

But it is evening.

Evening.

The levelling of the day,
a balance at the end of the afternoon.

★

Somehow,
they no longer fear the cold.
Single-paned windows collect vapours,
puddles at the sills. They go unwiped.

My parents leave a crack open
throughout the year

a fuzzed sweater
flung across the back of a chair
shapes itself to the wood.

When they release me,
a wind comes between us,
feels like a body, warm and live;
it says that it will come back,
that it comes from the north,
that it has to go.

★

When Em died,
she was placed in a white casket,
wearing violets across her throat,
heliotropes clasped in her hands.

She left instructions to have the pallbearers
take her out the back door,
through the garden and meadow
and straight into the cemetery
in order to avoid the eyes of strangers.

For Em, angels were earthbound,
heaven was found below.
After my visit, somewhere on Earth,
an angel discovered a planet without a star.

It just moves through thalassic hinterlands of space,
orbiting absolutely nothing,

and I'm relieved

to know that something so large
can still wander.

ENDNOTES

1 Traditionally, this poem would be written vertically, each line beginning from top to bottom, and moving from right to left. This particular form, called "the five-character-quatrain," is considered one of the hardest forms of Chinese poetry, as its aim is to convey the most meaning using a limited number of words, all the while obeying rules for rhyme, rhythm, tone, and balance.

2 William Carlos Williams, "An Approach to the Poem," in *English Institute Essays*, 1947 (New York: AMS Press, 1965), 68.

3 Ming Dong Gu, *Chinese Theories of Reading and Writing* (New York: State University of New York Press, 2005), 224.

4 Ibid.

5 Leonard Cohen, *20th Century Poetry & Poetics*, ed. Gary Geddes (Oxford University Press, 1973).

6 Jacques deLisle, "'One World, Different Dreams': The Contest to Defining the Beijing Olympics," in *Owning the Olympics: Narratives of the New China*, eds. Monroe E. Price and Daniel Dayan (University of Michigan Press, 2008), 35.

7 "China's 'Lucky' Phone Number," *BBC News*, August 19, 2003, web.

8 Catherine Abbott, *The Everything Small-Space Gardening Book* (Simon & Schuster, 2012).

9 *The Writer and His Roots*, produced by Joe MacDonald (NFB, 1983), film.

10 Nicole Brossard, "Poetic Politics," in *Fluid Arguments* (Mercury Press, 2005), 28.

11 Maggie Nelson, *The Argonauts* (Graywolf Press, 2015).

12 Ludwig Wittgenstein, *Tractatus Logico-Philosophicus*, trans. C. K. Ogden (Cosimo Classics, 2007).

13 Louise Glück, *Proofs and Theories* (Ecco, 1994), 3.

14 Rainer Maria Rilke, *The Notebooks of Malte Laurids Brigge* (Penguin, 2011), 19.

15 John Elderfield, *Cézanne Portraits* (Princeton University Press, 2017), 30.

16 Jeanette Winterson, *Art Objects: Essays on Ecstasy and Effrontery* (Vintage Canada, 1996), 3.

17 Isaac Kaplan, "How Long Do People Really Spend Looking at Art in Museums?" *Artsy* 7 (November 2017), web.

18 Barbara Y. Newsom and Adele Z. Silver, eds., *The Art Museum as Educator* (University of California Press, 1978), 81.

19 L. F. Smith, J. K. Smith, and P. P. L. Tinio, "Time spent viewing art and reading labels," *Psychology of Aesthetics, Creativity, and the Arts* 11, no. 1 (2017): 77-85.

20 John Berger, *Ways of Seeing* (Penguin Books, 1972), 9.

21 Winterson, *Art Objects*, 19.

22 Winterson, *Art Objects*, 4.

23 P. Adams Sitney, *Eyes Upside Down: Visionary Filmmakers and the Heritage of Emerson* (New York: Oxford University Press, 2008), 154.

24 *A Drownful Brilliance of Wings*, directed by Sofia Bohdanowicz (2016), short film, 8 min. The film, based on the poem "Arriving" from *Peeling Rambutan*, screened at a number of festivals across Canada, and in USA, China, Argentina, and Portugal.

25 Sylvia Plath, "Metaphors," *Collected Poems*, ed. Ted Hughes (London: Faber & Faber, 1981), 116.

26 Elizabeth Bishop, *Poems* (FSG, 2011), 68.

27 Sappho, *If Not, Winter: Fragments of Sappho*, trans. Anne Carson (New York: Vintage Books, 2002), 343.

28 Amy Lowell, *Selected Poems* (Library of America, 2004), 11.

29 Anne Sexton, *The Complete Poems* (Mariner Books, 1999), 299.

30 Zi Ye, *The Anchor Book of Chinese Poetry*, eds. Tony Barnstone and Chou Ping (Anchor Books, 2005), 64.

NOTES & ACKNOWLEDGEMENTS

Some of these poems and essays have been previously published, often in different forms and with different titles. Thank you to the editors of those publications: *Poetry Is Dead*, *Arc Poetry Magazine*, *Maisonneuve*, *carte blanche*, *LooseLeaf Magazine*, *Ricepaper Magazine*, and *Prairie Fire*.

"Fricatives (A Visit)" was published as a limited-edition chapbook in Gaspereau Press's *Devil's Whim Series*. It was translated into French by Luba Markovskaia and Daoud Najm and published in *ellipse*, Issue 90. Excerpts of Emily Dickinson are from *The Complete Poems of Emily Dickinson* (1976), *The Letters of Emily Dickinson* (2011), and *The Life and Letters of Emily Dickinson* (1972). "My father moved through dooms of love" is borrowed from E. E. Cummings.

"Fauna" was adapted into a short film, *Nocturne*, directed by Robert Huynh (Vancouver Film School).

"Ten Transitions" are creative translations of poems composed by my uncle Aldo Lam (who writes under the pen name 思恺).

"Current" is a poetic response to Shane Wilson's sculpture, *Gaia* (2009).

An earlier version of "The Hesitant Gaze" was presented at the Vanier College English Symposium (Montreal, Quebec) in November 2018.

★

I am grateful to the Conseil des arts et des lettres du Québec and the jurors for supporting this project. I also wish to thank Michael Holmes, Emily Schultz, and the team at ECW for their careful and insightful edits.

Deepest appreciation to my family, who shared and trusted me with their stories, especially my beloved Ah Ma, Aldo Lam, Steven Zhang, Katherine Lam, Mark Lam, Leigh Chang, and my parents. I am indebted to them for their generosity and love.

Heartfelt thanks to: my teachers and students for giving me the opportunities to learn from them; my dear friends, whose conversations about motherhood, poetry, and art buoyed me; my earliest companions Edmond and Edwin; and my parents for giving me this world and these eyes. To Manish Sharma: I cannot think of a better partner with whom to be entangled. Infinite, infinite love to Aalok and Eider. You two have given me the best of all possible significations.

This book is also available as a Global Certified Accessible™ (GCA) ebook. ECW Press's ebooks are screen reader friendly and are built to meet the needs of those who are unable to read standard print due to blindness, low vision, dyslexia, or a physical disability.

At ECW Press, we want you to enjoy our books in whatever format you like. If you've bought a print copy just send an email to ebook@ecwpress.com and include:

- the book title
- the name of the store where you purchased it
- a screenshot or picture of your order/receipt number and your name
- your preference of file type: PDF (for desktop reading), ePub (for a phone/tablet, Kobo, or Nook), mobi (for Kindle)

A real person will respond to your email with your ebook attached. Please note this offer is only for copies bought for personal use and does not apply to school or library copies.

Thank you for supporting an independently owned Canadian publisher with your purchase!